Poetry from the Heart

To Jodie!
You are an awesome
woman thank you so
much for inspiring me to
push my Art farther
and here we are!
Love,
Angel

Poetry from the Heart

*Poems inspired by the practice of Nichiren Daishonin's Buddhism
in the Soka Gakkai International*

by Angel Latterell
including poems by other Bodhisattvas of the Earth

This collection of poems is dedicated to Tsunesaburo Makiguchi, Josei Toda, Daisaku Ikeda and all Lion-hearted disciples & mentors standing up for the sake of Kosen-rufu.

Acknowledgements

For allowing me to include their words and poems in this book I would like to thank specifically Jodie Knowles my co-writer on "Open my Life" and Misty Dawn Spicer co-poet on "November 18" writing part two "Justice". The following individuals performed and contributed to the poem "Perseverance" as part of the very first West Territory Spoken Word Corp:

Raphael Briscoe
Brooke Benson
Misty-Dawn Spicer
Jose Albillo
Katie Anderson
Andrew Steiner
George Steiner
Khepra Ptah
Kyle Andreson
Mark Morales
Danielle Jackson
Karla Towers
Ryan Hayashi
Kerry Breuer
Kelly Dunlap
Shawn Aubrey

Deanna Montez
Nathalie Parras
J.C.
Lindsey Rodgers
Byrd Palec
Takashi (Tee)
Akira Yamamoto
Renita Sweed
Karlamaria Aguilar
Omar Tellez
Rod Jackson
Raphael Briscoe
Mike West
Lazarus Guindry

I would like to thank all of the performers who performed these poems with me over the years, specifically Lamar Lofton, Adrienne White, Flora McGill, Katy Webber, and Amber Flame.

Last but not least, for their encouragement of me over the years in faith, the following individuals I thank with utmost sincerity for helping begin and continue in my practice of buddhism: Megumi Yamasaki, Nicole Walters, Julia Russell, Martin Applebaum, Justine Piontek, Stephanie Araiza.

"More valuable than treasures in a storehouse are the treasures of the body, and the treasures of the heart are the most valuable of all. From the time you read this letter on, strive to accumulate the treasures of the heart!"

The Three Kinds of Treasure –
Writings of Nichiren Diashonin Volume 1 p. 851

"If our hearts are burning with hope and courage at all times and filled with the spirit of challenge, we'll be brimming with joy and vigor no matter what our situation. This is true happiness."

The New Human Revolution, Volume 22 –
Daisaku Ikeda

"Both peace and poetry resonate with the language of the heart."

The Poetry of Peace – David Krieger

Table of Contents

Determination Poem

I will be the lion's roar — song of victory.
I will be the new dawn golden sunlight illuminating
treasure tower faces until they lift their arms to welcome
each moment with joy.
Together - our voices shall be the shovel that unearth
bodhisattvas to stand as disciples living the shared vow
creating kosen-rufu from the stones of blue sky reality.

Perseverance

Rock the Era, Long Beach Culture Festival,
West Territory Spoken Word Corp – July 10, 2010

This is the Poem.
This is the Poem of my life.
I will persevere.
As disciples we reply
To never be defeated
Above the highest mountains we will fly
With a song of peace in our hearts and
determined prayer as our guide.

Golden Gate Mentor Disciple Zone

We are warriors of light fighting for peace
Conquering our devilish functions, slaying the beast
Our words for swords, powerful and heavy, not paper thin
Our practice is our shield, protection from within
We chant until our hearts feel full and reveal
Courage of a lion burning from within
Determined we chant
For kosen-rufu to begin!

Above the highest mountains we will fly
With a song of peace in our heart and
determined prayer as our guide.

Los Angeles Zone

We have a mission
No matter the obstacle
To strengthen the world condition
Replying to Sensei
We'll fight side by side,
Through any kind of weather
Rainstorms or shine
We'll climb peak by peak till we reach our true goal
Spreading world peace to every being we know
Let us persevere
When winter turns to spring
Bodhisattvas emerge without fear

Above the highest mountains we will fly
With a song of peace in our hearts and
determined prayer as our guide.

Los Angeles North Coast Zone

My heart pours Deep into the law
My friends I chant aimfully
With no flaw
Taking steps of sunshine
Devotion through my voice
I am that Lotus growing through the tar
You've seen the change
And it's as serene as the ocean
Or as violent as a hurricane

Above the highest mountains we will fly
With a song of peace in our hearts and
determined prayer as our guide.

Pacific Northwest Zone

I am the light I sought
The sulking clouds of doubt have evaporated
I am my own red gold sea
Join me
Stand by me
Just watch how powerful we can be
We fall
We rise again
We start anew
The valley of hope stands a tall monument
Dancing over the crest of each hill
Absolutely Victorious.

Above the highest mountains we will fly
With a song of peace in our hearts and
determined prayer as our guide.

San Francisco Ever Victorious Zone

This is the poem the poem of my life
Swimming against the currents of conflict
Running towards the sun rays of peace
Drumming through the battlefield of sorrow
Dancing my way to complete happiness
Determined to find the Buddha in me & the universe
Breaking all barriers
Hurtling toward our destiny
We emerge victorious
Fly like phoenix
Wings ablaze with courage
Never to be defeated.

Above the highest mountains we will fly
With a song of peace in our hearts and
determined prayer as our guide.

Southern California West Zone

We rely on wisdom instead of egotistical pride.
We will always strive for our opportunity to win and never
again allow the sneering grin of my evil twin.
So by fulfilling my impossible dream,
I will keep my head afloat above the oceans of negativity
The Time is now to uplift those who are defeated
Don't hesitate bring it home with faith.
When hope is low it's time to breakthrough and grow

No matter what I will persevere
The devil king has no place here
Our practice is our shield
Protection from within
With the courage of a lion king let victory begin.

Open My Life

Test the Truth of Buddhism Now!
The Musical – January 31, 2010

Seattle North and Seattle Urban Youth Division
Jodie Knowles & Angel Latterell

Sensho.

Nam myoho renge kyo
Nam myoho renge kyo
Nam myoho renge kyo

me

Open my life
Unlock the insecure
Break fist clenching dreams
Press palms together and breathe

us

Open my life
Expand arms so wide
True worth becomes the sky

Her

My life coulda been a pebble
A stone underfoot
Drifting and bouncing
A calamity ride where you wake up on the other side
Not knowin' the path back or forward

us (But then I heard this word) *chant*

Heard the sound of consonants mix with vowels
The song of my life entered these ears

us **Nam myoho renge kyo**

me

Breath your life into the mystic law
Tell it to open you
Tell it to pull out your innate beauty

6

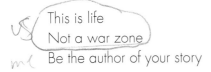

This is life
Not a war zone
Be the author of your story

Nam myoho renge kyo

Took my tiny life
And broke it open
Breathed it open
Burned it open
Unlocked potential
Until the pebble became a continent

Nam myoho renge kyo

Open my life
Unlock the insecure
Break fist clenching dreams
Press palms together and breathe

Open my life
Expand arms so wide
True worth becomes the sky

Nam myoho renge kyo

This is not a genie!
It's the power of your life
merge with the truth
it's your time to rise

It's a matter of hearing ourselves
A matter of listening to wisdom's soft voice
Sometimes hiding in the closet from our
fundamental darkness

We got it all dressed up like ET tryin' to be something
it was never meant to be
When the true nature is right there when we breathe
And it will ALWAYS be stronger than our weakness

Nam myoho renge kyo

Open your eyes to your truth
Polish your mirror
Chant with your heart
Open your chest
Let the burning of your desires
Keep your feet moving forward

Nam myoho renge kyo

It's a fiery lantern that no cavern can defeat
Turn it on and the light will shine the way
Your life is just waiting for you to flip on that switch

Nam myoho renge kyo
Nam myoho renge kyo
Nam myoho renge kyo

A brilliant burning sun

Pacific Northwest Spoken Word Corp
May 2010

A brilliant burning sun
Rises above the new land.
Over a bright shining horizon
A gleaming car pulls up
Carrying the Bodhisattvas of the Earth.
Plowing through obstacles,
Horsepower unparalleled,
Burning rubber
While blazing a trail behind us
In tire smoke
Lighting the way for others.

Off in the distance
There may be those that criticize us
With wane foolish sarcastic smiles
But our hearts are armor
With shields of steel
Never to be defeated any evil
Or envy.
Not to surcome to our devilish functions
Of greed, anger, and foolishness
It is hard,
But defeat is not an option.

So we dance in the light of hope
And those that look upon us smile with joy.
Like a butterfly we spread our wings and advance
Transforming karma in our wake.
Nod-a cad-a-pila no mo

Emerged from our cocoons of fear
Forget the rut I'm not stuck.

Now is the time to vigorously sing a song
Of the springtime of peace.
We don't need beats
We spread peace
Every time we meet
Through the streets.
We move
Spreading rhythms of shakabuku
Letting you know
You can do it too!

Messenger of Hope

Seattle Area Women's Division Meeting – February 2006
Poem performed by Angel Latterell with Adrienne White dancing

To be a messenger of hope,
We must be the spark
from the wet stone
that first made fire.
We must be the will to climb higher.
The first to jump into mired
conversation until
common ground is found.

To be a messenger of hope,
We must be the smile
on a child's eye.
Sunlight twinkling
from cold skyscraper.
Soft words in hard conversation.
A community knit from
cracks of fragmentation.
A colorful kite flying
into future skies
And the child asking why.

As the harbingers of hope
fighting for the absolute happiness
of every human being,
we are here to celebrate life.
Awakening from the monotony
to see the potential of all humanity
to be free from the pains of
birth and death.

The struggle of existence
is built from the resistance
of individuals to trust.
It's material things or bust,
filling the void of uncertainty
with quests for control,
making this journey a toll road,
instead of discovering
the middle way
where bodhisattvas play
and dance as emissaries
of compassion.

So today we are here
to appreciate the life that is
the blood in our veins.
The same life that
brings the rains
and the sun's rays
sending each of us
on our way
ready to experience the
true nature of all phenomena.
Awake to the light
of three thousand realms
of existence in a single moment.

My hand is the sun.
Your heart the water
that feeds the thirsty.
You and I are both
children of the sky
and fish swim through
our body.

Existence is merely the form
even though it swarms us
day by day until there appears
to be no other way out
but a casket.
When our real task in life
is to see the true essence,
being the best human being
we can be,
putting that feeling of darkness
trapping us in this flesh
to rest with that blanket of hopelessness
peeled from sleeping eyes
so we may know hope with our lives
and win the battle over despair.

Like a trumpet song blares
above the cacophony
a messenger of hope
must play that note for others.
Taking up the rope
to show the way
with daily life
becoming actual proof
that joy is not fleeting,
but a constant state
when we appreciate
everything we encounter.

To be messengers of hope
we must sing compassion
with every breath
even though the path
is wrought with obstacles.

But our team has many talents
one mind but many bodies
equals boundless creativity
that will make
all impossibility
actual reality!

"At the time of kosen rufu all people in the entire world will become votaries of the Lotus Sutra."

– Nichiren Diashonin

Jiyu Sun

Aurora District, Minnesota Area
November District General Meeting – 1999

In the morning
When the Jiyu Sun arises
We give the universe praises
Restoring our debt of gratitude
Gaining fortitude for the journey ahead
Learning to tread the path
Of mentor disciple
Helping people become aware
Of what's already there
Within the depths of their lives

In the morning
When the Jiyu Sun arises
A lion shall roar
In celebration of courage
As we work to scourge
Hell from this earth
Begin to bring rebirth
Through culture
Turning a sepulcher of suffering
Into fertilizer for a garden of joy
Dispersing seeds for the pollination of understanding

In the morning
When the Jiyu sun arises
Bodhisattvas will open their eyes
Upon the skies

Their dreams will create
Working for humanity
Restoring dignity to life
Helping each other to end strife
Stopping the knife
Of violence before it cuts
Healing the wound of war shut

In the morning
When the Jiyu Sun arises
We shall actualize limitless potential
Make a substantial commitment
To our community
As an ambassador of unity
Exerting ourselves bravely
Vigorously making the law
Universally known

In the morning
We shall start in the moment
Awakening to the light
Of a dawn that will continue
On until humanity finds it way
In the daylight of the Jiyu Sun

Awake

April Kosen Rufu Gongyo – 2010
Seattle Metro Region – Seattle North Area
Angel Latterell & piano

One person awake is the wave
that stirs the ocean of sleeping souls
until their hearts grow legs and dance onto the beach
to bring unceasing warmth to all the lands
where Buddhas may be.

We emerged dancing to the rhythm of the universe
and the great poem tells of this song that moved us
until the vow sprung up through the souls of our feet
into ankles, knees, hips, stomach, esophagus-
pranced to our tongue
and sprang from our mouth as
Nam myoho renge kyo.

Every time a new bodhisattva remembers this vow
they awake from beneath the dirt of the present day swamp
causing a rumble in the earth
until their Buddha form emerges
spreading its arms wide
singing a trapeze of lotus flower limbs
until just the right moment then
JUMP
another one arrives feet aflare
to the unmistakable golden glow of rhythm
from time without beginning

(A11) until the world looks like the ceremony in the air
elevated above the fields of failure
elated in the air of determined feet
moving always to an incessant rhythm
that can sing nothing but the power of fundamental happiness.

I woke up one day
My life became a light beam
Enunciated through sound
My voice singing the name to unlock all doors
(A11) Nam myoho renge kyo
This awakening opened my eyes
To see the crystal clear geyser of appreciation
To draw water from hope refreshment
Filling every single cell of my being with golden energy
To spring forward on tiger legs
towards that victory
waiting patiently for me to actualize it.

There can be moments of doubt
where that step forward becomes a cliff jump
(A11) but our faith gives us wings
that can fly on hope alone.

The demon king's armies are sneaky
They pose as self talk
Ill intentioned friends
Conflicts of interest
Annoying people
As sisters and brothers and fellow believers

We must strip them bare
of their costume armor with
our prayers
(All) DECLARE
Nothing will stop us from achieving our goals
me Nothing will stop us from helping another who is suffering
Nothing will stop us!
(All) Nothing will stop us!
Not even the demon king himself.

(All) Nam myoho renge kyo

Nichiren Daishonin will be our model of fearlessness
Daisaku Ikeda our mentor on how to win
(All) We shall never doubt
Never let the night be separated
from the dawn of
the new day
Where each moment we learn our way with joy
in the practice we were so lucky to encounter.

(All) Nam myoho renge kyo
I am awake
I am dancing
I will win
Because I will never give up.

19

Joy Smell

For Gohonzon Conferral Encouragement – June 2007

The first time I smelled joy
it came with the sound of my voice singing –

nam myoho renge kyo

Kitchen stove simmering ginger,
glowing from my lungs in song
a thousand kalpas long.
Bringing future bodhisattvas
treasures of cinnamon bark medicine,
to dance from tongue to heart.

I awoke with a start –
gunpowder sulfur smell in the room
the scent of a candle burning 700 years.

nam myoho renge kyo

Written by Nichiren Diashonin in sumi ink.
Gave my blind eyes their first glimpse
of lilac scented sun on telescope parchment.
Opening the door to the storehouse hidden,
even to those with two good eyes.

Medicine King whose operations leave scars of victory
shining in starlight smiles of faith –
where poison once was.

nam myoho renge kyo

Curing the dead and the living.
Every being can benefit from its song.
Mercury streamer lantern kisses,
blessing the masses as they weave and dip along
the rhythm.

nam myoho renge kyo

The note is there within waiting for release from the lips.
Making the cause with body & heart,
directing mind beyond time & space.
To the place without beginning or end,
where the candles has been lit – waiting to start the fire
of a thousand lands of Buddha wonder,
unfolding beneath our noses, yearning to smell joy.

November 18

Seattle Metro Region Kosen Rufu Gongyo –
November 7, 2010

Seattle Metro Region Spoken Word Corp
presentation on Discussion Meetings and
the Significance of November 18

Angel Latterell & Misty Dawn Spicer

I.   Mentor & Disciple

On November 18, 1945
at the memorial for his mentor Makiguchi,
Toda the lion stood alone at the precipice.
His body wracked with illness,
he alone spoke for the mission his mentor died defending.

Just as Shigo Kingo held the reigns of Nichiren's horse
as they walked toward their execution,
Toda walked with Makiguchi.
Said – I will go with you to the ends of the earth.
Makiguchi,
with the heart of Nichiren,
stood to remonstrate the Japanese government and
its war machine.
He said – Toda will you go with me?
Toda did, and everyone else forsake them
for fear of authority.
Everyone traded in their lion king beards
for coward robes.
Only Makiguchi and Toda,
united at the heart,
took on the government for the sake of the people.

As Nikko Shonin & Nichiren Diashonin said before them –
Do not following even the High Priest if he should espouse
his own views above the Mystic Law.

Makiguchi's spirit to put his heart in the same place as
Nichiren's is the cause for which we all stand here today.
He said – Toda we must remonstrate for the sake of the
people – we cannot let the government force the Shinto
talisman on our members.
Only thru Nam myoho renge kyo will Japan find peace.
For the sake of the land Shinto must be refused.

His direct disciple saw that spirit & heart,
he accepted the responsibility to follow his mentor into hell.
And they both found Shakymuni Buddha there.

November is the month of disciples hearts.
November is the month when the lion king roars and cowards run.
November is the month where the strong take the
heart of the mentor as their own
and the future opens up
from the cause of Nam myoho renge kyo.
The Mystic Law – cause of all causes is uttered by 10 thousand
bodhisattvas witnessing the shared mission with their voice.
Speaking out for the sake of the happiness & security
of all humanity.

November is the month where there is a disciple taking action.

Nichiren stood on behalf of the mystic law
He was not quiet
He did not wait for permission
He stood alone
Lion roaring for the sake of the law of life.
Makiguchi stood against the Japanese government
Roaring for the sake of the law.

Toda stood alone lion among men.
Just as Nikko Shonin did,
Toda too would bring his mentor's mission to life
in the wake of Makiguchi's mortal death.
Death would be triumphed over
in the spark of a disciple's heart.
In the willingness to stand tall,
strong, courageous, just as their mentor.
So we all stand here today because someone stood up.
Because Makiguchi went to prison
with the heart of Nichiren Diashonin in his own chest.
So today each and every single one of us can experience joy.

On August 14, 1947
Toda was united with his own disciple Daisaku Ikeda,
who took his spirit beyond the boundaries of Japan
to our doorstep.
We are here because these men gave their lives for the
sake of Nam myoho renge kyo.

November is a memorial for their lives
and our time to honor them.
By standing up each one of us
to say we shall never begrudge our lives
we will make the joy of ourselves and others the
highest priority.
True joy felt in the camaraderie of the stand alone spirit.
The lion pack does not follow
anything but the heart of the lion king
and that is not to follow but to lead.

To walk directly into that dark cave
because we know there is no way to bring light to its caverns
then by the glow of our shining heart.
Illuminating the path of mentor disciple
from the distant past into the innumerable future.

– Angel Latterell

II.   Justice

nikko shonin. HE stood up in the face of
adversity he displayed oneness with mentor,
turned his faith into action.

for the sake of spreading the LAW
for the sake of PEACE above all.
despite resistance from shinto priests:
he KNEW
a time will come in the name of peace

the length of a robe does not measure faith in your heart
for that very robe is what can tear us apart

for hundreds of years we were buried in timelined tradition
until together we stood up to face excommunication
and together we said THANK YOU! this is OUR justification

we will take the responsibility to win
we will stand for kosen rufu
that's what its about.
this FAIITH
this universe.
this NATION

this room
these PEOPLE
THIS moment.
If we ALL seek within and then
we ALL gain something from it.

that something could be happiness
that something could be PEACE.
that something is our own significance
right here at eagle peak.

nikko shonin turned his faith into action.
It built upon the FOUNDATION.
that makiguchi would later take to FRUTATION.
when presenting his pedegogy to the japanese NATION.

ALL in november...
such a significant month to remember

makiguchi,
he also turned faith into action.
november 18th 80 years prior.

makiguchi made his vow
and the entire cause
which brings us together NOW.

and when he died that same day
13 years later
toda knew the vow MUST continue.
and president ikeda stepped into the mission.

HE taught us person to person in any situation
brings about our true buddha nature.
this is the seed from which we grow.
A discussion meeting opens not only your home.

it is our ENTIRE heart.
OUR tolerance.
OUR opportunity to remember.
IT IS our fortune
to have study,
to have dialogue,
and to practice right HERE,
together.

– Misty Dawn Spicer

Born Again

Northern Pioneers District Meeting
Minnesota Area – 2004

I was born again today
old Karma washed away
skeletons in the closet
packed up and sent to Goodwill
with those pants I haven't fit in years
and the future is clearer than
tea leaves in the bottom of my cup
cuz I was born again today
not in some Christian way
I just let the bags drop
where I last walked
didn't look back
just gave up being
the little engine that could
embraced the lack of freight behind me
and trudged right up the hill
to see that the grass
was actually greener on the other side
my empty closets gleam potential
for a new wardrobe of life
wrapping only light around my eyes
to dispel the gloom of learned frustration
in exchange for elation
in the act of breathing
watching squirrels dance in the trees
people crossing streets
enjoying my cake and eating it too
born again today
not to repent
but to no longer be
pent up energy

Hope Stoplight

Intersection: A Spoken Word Opera
December 7 & 8, 2007

Angel Latterell & Ensemble of musicians and dancers

Words sometimes fail me
when the glimmer of time sparkles on wet streets.
Car headlights too bright in dilated pupils –
moments pass in glimpses stole from camera shutters,
digitalized on cartridges not as reliable as our computers.
We can only breathe and smile
hoping bugs won't mar our teeth too much.

A match stick away from nothing,
release will find us at the end of this sidewalk,
where you can cross –
or wait your whole life for the walk sign
telling you it is safe to go.
Death will happen before the red light ends.

Hope is not fashion, nor a yellow light of caution.
It is what makes one foot move in front of the other
every single day.

Until you no longer have feet – then if you are still alive,
its momentum will carry you to a place
where a new pair will be provided for you.

Revolution

Seattle Metro Region Kosen Rufu Gongyo
December 2005
Angel Latterell & Lamar Lofton on Bass

So you say you want a Revolution, well you know, we all want
to change the world. . .

Revolution:
word not born from strife,
but evolution,
stolen from astronomy,
meaning first,
celestial movement
goin' on & on & on & on. . . .
planetary motion around the sun
equals one Revolution.
So Revolution became,
sudden momentous change.
Strong word, heard round the world,
the barrel of a gun
through the boom of a cannon
the sssssssssshhhhhhhhwap!
of the Guillotine,
as Revolution exchanged
one government for another.

Revolution:
holy mother of words
holding the fate of
humanity in her syllables.
Embodying fundamental change
of values, institutions, leadership
both societal and political, not partial
as there can be no coup de taut of hope

no rebellion of happiness.
The firebombs will fall until
the Revolution for all humanity
comes to fruition as each individual
takes complete responsibility
for the Revolution they wish to see.

Let there be peace on Earth,
and let it begin with Me!

Revolution:
strong enough sentiment
for people to lay down their lives,
but can we create a Revolution for life?
It takes resolute determination
to lead ourselves,
let alone the nation
towards transformation
where change is not so sudden
but subtle like evolution.
Bringin' Revolution back
to its original meaning
only this time not around
but towards the rising sun
of a future
where we have only begun
to explore peace.

So true Revolution
becomes a choice between meanings.
Do we continue practicing
Darwanism by gun
Revolution via missile?
Forgetting that each human being
is the ultimate vessel of systemic change?

Or, do we change?
It's our choice.
Our Human Revolution,
that will transform our environment
one person at a time
until we all resolve to be
many in body but one in mind
and find finally an answer to the question.
Cuz its not,
gonna be alright. . .alright
until we learn that the
ultimate path is within
and that is where
Revolution must begin.

Can I Write a Rhyme?

Building Bridges of Peace
Minnesota Area Summer Youth Culture Festival
August 2000

Can I write a rhyme
to help change this time
into a place where a line
of poetry will make
people look into themselves
take their life from the shelves
of corporate slavery
consumer mediocrity
Hollywood morality
and begin to behave
how they ought to be
realizing the interconnected
actuality of reality
the causality of all action
no longer faction themselves
into groups based on difference.

I want to write a rhyme
that will create an outbreak of peace
break our lease on war
stop making humanity the whore
of violence and silence
perpetuated by fear
wondering why we are here
if not to draw near to our death.
Let's take a breath
speak to the Buddhanature
of our brother
no longer smother ourselves

in worthless negativity.
Can I write a rhyme
that will buy us more time
so that we may find
a home within ourselves
stop three thousand realms of hell
from descending upon earth
to hurt the children of our children
the brethren of our human family.

Let's talk of our future
in order to suture
the bonds of humanity
begin to bring sanity
to our synthetic electronically
transmitted community
making unity from futility
bringing agility to fragility
humility to anger and greed
so we may fulfill that need
that we must heed
before we do a deed
that will lead to our destruction.
Let's begin to function as a whole
begin to see the goal of our existence.

I want to write a rhyme
that will build a bridge across boundaries
because I cannot point fingers and take sides.
I cannot pretend I know quantitatively
more than you know about this world.
I cannot forget that it is possible
to learn from others,
that there are different viewpoints to be heard
coming from different understandings of this life.
I will not critique and

I will not seek a scapegoat.
Why must I draw lines
and stifle all meaningful debate
when it is arguments that continue to breed hate?
I must work to bring the principles
in conflict out of the confusion and dirt
understanding that everyone is hurt
by our inability to resolve issues that involve
differing perceptions of reality.

I must understand that change
starts with myself.
My ability to communicate.
My ability to facilitate dialogue.
My ability to create change
in my own environment.
I must break the chain
begin to heal the pain
realize how much everyone
will stand to gain
if we open up the channels of
compassionate cooperative interaction
and no longer faction
ourselves into groups based on difference.

I will build a bridge from you to me
a bridge from me to you
and start to do
something
to create peace.

Blood of the Buddha

Sandpoint District, Seattle North Area
Women's Meeting – February 2008

What does buddhahood smell like?
What does buddhahood taste like?
What does it taste like?
I'm hungry. What do I eat?

Buddhahood is -
the heart of compassion
the mind of wisdom
the body of courageous action.
It is never lying down until the fight is done
the battle won with internal darkness.
It is holding the torch to light the way through
murky passages for others.

So it smells like sulfur.
Sulfur fire burning on the biofuel
of karmic obstacles-
the tool to keep the way lit bright & clear
for others to find their own way to happiness.

It tastes like blood.
The blood in your veins when you bite your tongue
because it is in there – every drop of it is Buddha
your body when you act for others is Buddha
your body when you act for the sake of the law is Buddha.

Buddhahood tastes of the salt in your sweat as you
make progress everyday to practice the way.
It is the treat of sweet effort extracted
from the honeysuckle vine - the result of
pulling earnestly from within the thing
which shall be secret no longer.

Buddhahood smells like the wind
rustling the papers of your mind disorganizing the piles of
"this must be this way" and "that must be that"
and "change is impossible" or impossibly hard.

Your life is the Buddha waiting to be released
from within to roar so loud that the chimes lulling
you into complacency hide waking
your mind
your senses
your eyes
to see
to hear
to smell the sulfur
to taste the blood of the Buddha
who is you.

The Second Act Begins

*Our Golden Autumn: Ablaze with the Passion &
Power of Youth — October 9 –10, 2010*

*Youth Culture Festival — 50th Anniversary of
SGI President Ikeda's visit to Seattle*

*Angel Latterell & Pacific Northwest Zone Ikeda
Youth Ensemble Spoken Word Corp*

50 years ago I stepped alone off the shore of Japan
with nothing but a dream
held inside the contents of a travel bag
To introduce the world to Nam myoho renge kyo.

I said I would do it to show appreciation for my mentor
To honor the man that showed me
thru the heart & the spirit
there is nothing impossible.
My heart should strive to be even more expansive than his.

My 32 year old shoes stepped
across the water of the Pacific Ocean
into an example for the world
that Nam myoho renge kyo knows no boundaries
it is the key to the most expansive state of life.

In my hands was a golden baton,
holding the keys to a future
when the sun rises on a land of peace and kosen rufu.
All we have to do is actualize it
with determination.

I have carried the baton for 50 years
without doubt
without concern that my successors would be ready at
the vital moment
when the 2nd Act is ready to begin.

All the world is a stage
And I have been the lead actor since 1960
Writing my story in the glorious print of victory
for all the world to see.
Now it's your turn youth.

Today. 50 years since I stepped off that airplane
with nothing but my heart in a travel bag
and the determined spirit to win on my sleeve.

Now it is your turn to take this baton
and bring this world into the 2nd Act.
Where kosen rufu is not a dream but reality
built by the actions of your brilliant shining hearts.

There was just one of me.
There are millions of you.
Believe more than doubt can take away.
Be the treasure tower of tomorrow.
You are center stage for the second act.

The era is already rocking from the rhythm of
your generation's
bodhisattva wings emerging from the earth.
Now own it with your entire being.
Never hesitate a moment to Dance!

"The teachings of the Lotus Sutra are like this. When in one's heart one takes faith in Nam myoho renge kyo, the heart becomes a dwelling and Shakyamuni Buddha takes up residence there. At first one is not aware of this, but gradually, as the months go by, the Buddha in the heart begins to appear as in a dream, and one's heart become bit by bit ever more joyful."

The Buddha Resides in a Pure Heart
The Writings of Nichiren Diashonin Volume II p. 885

My Debt of Gratitude: The Story of my Practice

In September of 1996 I moved to St. Paul, Minnesota to attend college at Macalester. During orientation I was handed a pamphlet listing local religious organizations. Curious about Buddhism I turned to the page listing Buddhist temples and organizations. The SGI-USA St. Paul/Minneapolis Community Center phone number was at the top of the list. I called it and a woman answered the phone. I said "Hi, my name is Angel and I would like to learn about Buddhism." The woman took my phone number and name and said that she would have someone call me back.

Within one or two days a young woman named Megumi called me to ask if I would like to meet her to discuss her practice. We met soon thereafter in a coffee shop by my school. She and another young woman named Nicole brought some notepaper and a pen and they spent the next hour telling me about practice of Nichiren's Buddhism as practiced by the Soka Gakkai International. Nicole drew a picture of a beaker and talked about how chanting stirs up the sentiment of our life so we can change our karma and become happy. They told me about Nichiren Diashonin, Nam myoho renge kyo, the ten worlds and the daily practice of chanting in your home every morning and evening. At the end of our discussion and dialogue I shared with them that this was exactly the type of Buddhist practice I was looking for because it applied to my daily life. I asked them, "When can I learn to chant?"

Two days later, Nicole took me to her home and she and Megumi chanted with me and demonstrated Gongyo (the name for chanting the "expedient means" and "life span" chapters of the Lotus Sutra every morning and evening). I chanted Nam myoho renge kyo for the first time. Megumi gave me a Gongyo book and a set of pink prayer beads that she had used that day. I went home and began to chant. I was so intent on learning Gongyo that I went to the music practice rooms at the fine arts center so that I would not disturb my three dorm room roommates. In two weeks I had learned Gongyo.

Megumi, my Area Young Women's Division leader, called me at least weekly to tell me about meetings and chanting opportunities. She came to visit me at my dorm room to chant with me. I said yes to every opportunity to chant. Chanting was the best thing I ever encountered – it made me feel happy and I didn't even know what the words meant. Megumi introduced me to my Women's Division District Leader Julia. Julia called me every week to remind about the district meeting, district tosos (chanting meetings) and just to make sure I knew I could come and chant at her house with her anytime.

In two months I asked – "How do I receive a Gohonzon?" Megumi said that if I practiced with my district consistently for the next three months and subscribed to publications she would sponsor me to receive my Gohonzon. I was already receiving the World Tribune and Seikyo Times which I read ravenously along with my packed college course load. So I was very excited to know that I could get my Gohonzon in March. March 7, 1997 I received my very own Gohonzon. [To receive Gohonzon is to become a member of the Soka Gakkai International and to receive the scroll first inscribed by Michiren Daishonin depicting with words the state of Buddhahood in a person's life.]

One month later I started receiving counseling for my eating disorder after having a breakthrough chanting in front of the Gohonzon. I never looked back from that moment. I have been able to do this because of the support of my youth leaders and my Men's and Women's Division District Leaders who worked as a family to raise me to be the capable person that I am today. Every place I have been in this organization there was a youth leader and a district leader there for me encouraging me to continue and to challenge my life. If those individuals did not call me every week, or encouraged me to chant and study, I know that my practice would not be as strong as it is today.

Poetry and Buddhism

In 1997, I went to my first poetry slam and I saw courageous poets on stage submitting their art to the judgment of the crowd. That next year, 1998, I attended a large gathering of the Central Zone SGI – USA Buddhists at the Chicago Culture Center. Two young men got on stage and did a spoken word piece about Buddhism. I determined at that moment that I would become a spoken word poet. I was already a poet, but my poems were short and descriptive and didn't translate into performance pieces. I determined that I was going to perform on stage, compete in poetry slams and I was going to share Buddhism with my words.

I began to chant about this and immediately began to write poetry for performance and about my Buddhist practice.

I won my first poetry slam in February of 1999, and I made it to the Minnesota Grand Slam in 2000. In the meantime I went to the 1999 Grand Youth Culture Festival in Los Angeles. I went with 3 fellow youth members. It was my first time on the West Coast – in Los Angeles where all of the SGI Buddhists were! And they performed on a grand stage in front of me. I said – "We are going to do this in Minnesota." I returned and proposed that Minnesota Area hold a culture festival – all of the youth there were so excited. The Men's and Women's Division supported us and in August of 2000 we performed "Building Bridges of Peace." It was my first collaborative performance piece featuring one of the poems in this book. Since that time I have volunteered for any meeting where I can use my poetry to encourage others.

In February of 2010 I was asked to be a Territory leader for the West Territory Rock the Era Youth Culture Festival for the Spoken Word Corp by our West Territory YWD Leader. I was so honored that I could reply to SGI President Daisaku Ikeda (a poet himself) by leading poets from across the Territory to work together to encourage others. The result, 5 months later myself and 32 other poets stood on stage and performed our collaborative piece "Perseverance" (in this book) in front of 20,000 people at the Long Beach Arena. My determination to be a spoken word artist for Buddhism had blossomed into actual proof beyond my wildest imagination.

In October 2010 I was able to work with a team of amazing youth to write and direct Northwest Zone's youth culture festival celebrating the 50th Anniversary of President Ikeda's visit to Seattle. I know now that 2010 was just the beginning of my journey to become a performance poet. My mission is to encourage the world with my words and to help others practice this Buddhism with joy.

Thank you to every person who encouraged my practice of this Buddhism since September of 1996. I compiled this book of poetry as an offering to repay my debt of gratitude to every single individual who made a cause allowing me to begin practicing this Buddhism and every person who encouraged me to continue.

Nam myoho renge kyo

Poetry is sculpted inner truth,
The flaring flame of earnestness.
An offering of poetry is an offering of life.

– Daisaku Ikeda

Made in the USA
Charleston, SC
29 March 2011